Weather Watchers

Clouds

Cassie Mayer

www.heinemann.co.uk/library
Visit our website to find out more information about Heinemann Library books.

To order:
 Phone 44 (0) 1865 888066
Send a fax to 44 (0) 1865 314091
 Visit the Heinemann Bookshop at www.heinemann.co.uk/library to browse our
catalogue and order online.

First published in Great Britain by Heinemann Library,
Halley Court, Jordan Hill, Oxford OX2 8EJ, part of Harcourt
Education. Heinemann is a registered trademark of Harcourt
Education Ltd.

© Harcourt Education Ltd 2007
First published in paperback in 2007
The moral right of the proprietor has been asserted.

Editorial: Tracey Crawford, Cassie Mayer, Dan Nunn,
and Sarah Chappelow
Design: Jo Hinton-Malivoire
Picture Research: Tracy Cummins, Tracey Engel,
and Ruth Blair
Production: Duncan Gilbert

Originated by Chroma Graphics (Overseas) Pte. Ltd
Printed and bound in China by South China
Printing Company

ISBN 978 0 431 18258 2 (hardback)
11 10 09 08 07
10 9 8 7 6 5 4 3 2 1

ISBN 978 0 431 18375 6 (paperback)
12 11 10 09 08
10 9 8 7 6 5 4 3 2 1

British Library Cataloguing in Publication Data
Mayer, Cassie
Clouds. - (Weather watchers)
1.Clouds - Juvenile literature
I.Title
551.5'76

Acknowledgements
The publishers would like to thank the following for permission
to reproduce photographs: Corbis pp. 4 (sunshine, G. Schuster/
zefa; rain, Anthony Redpath), 5, 12 (W. Cody), 13 (Royalty Free),
16 (Randy Wells), 17 (zefa/Herbert Spichtinger), 18 (Ronald
Thompson; Frank Lane Picture Agency), 19 (Darrell Gulin), 20
(Onne van der Wal), 21 (Craig Tuttle), 23 (Craig Tuttle); Getty
Images pp. 4 (lightning; snow, Marc Wilson Photography), 14
(Alan R. Moller), 15 (Johannes Kroemer).

Cover photograph reproduced with permission of Jupiter Images
(thinkstock Images). Back cover photograph reproduced with
permission of Corbis (W. Cody).

Every effort has been made to contact copyright holders of any
material reproduced in this book. Any omissions will be rectified in
subsequent printings if notice is given to the publishers.

Contents

What is weather?

There are many types of weather.
Weather changes all the time.

A cloudy day is a type of weather.

What are clouds?

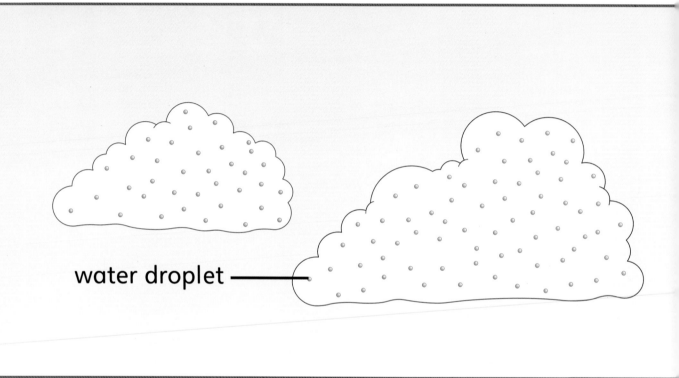

water droplet

Clouds are made of tiny drops of water.
These are called water droplets.

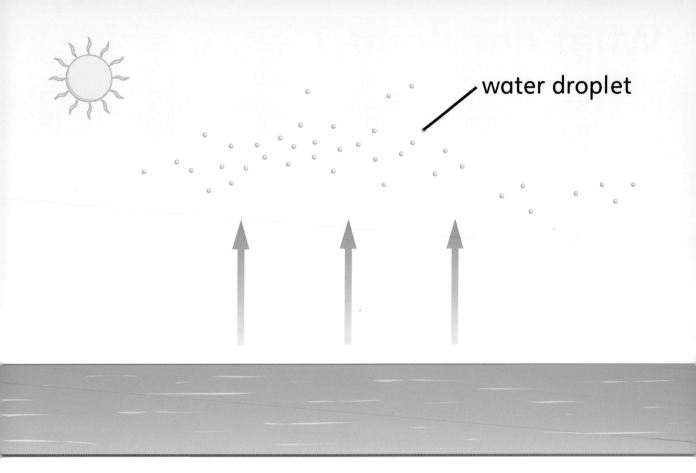

water droplet

When the sun warms water, some
of the water becomes vapour.
Vapour is air that is full of moisture.

Water vapour rises into the air. As it cools it forms water droplets. These water droplets make clouds.

raindrop

In the clouds, the droplets join together. They form raindrops.

The raindrops fall from the clouds.

Raindrops bring water to the earth.

Types of clouds

Some clouds are fluffy and white. You may see these clouds on a sunny day.

Some clouds are thick and grey. You may see these clouds on a rainy day.

Some clouds are big and dark. You may see these clouds on a stormy day.

Some clouds cover the sky. You may
see these clouds on a snowy day.

Some clouds are high.

Some clouds are low.

Some clouds are funny shapes.

Sometimes you see many
types of cloud at once.

How do clouds help us?

Living things need water to grow.
Clouds bring rain to the land.

Clouds help us predict the weather.

Cloud watching

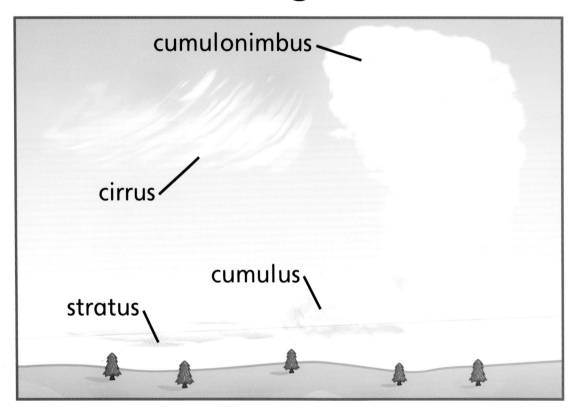

cumulonimbus

cirrus

cumulus

stratus

These are types of clouds.
Look for these clouds in the sky.

Picture glossary

predict to guess what will happen

raindrop a big drop of water

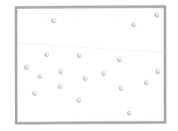

water droplet a tiny drop of water

Index

Notes to parents and teachers

Before reading

Talk about different weather. Ask the children which type of weather they like best. Have they ever looked at the clouds? Look at the clouds now and talk about what weather they might bring.

After reading

Sing this song to the tune of "Twinkle twinkle, little star": When I look into the sky, I can see the clouds go by, They don't ever make a sound, Floating high above the ground. Some go fast and some go slow, I wonder where the clouds all go.

Make a water cycle picture showing sunshine, water, clouds, and raindrops.

Create a "Clouds dance drama": Tell the story of a sequence of weather and ask the children to move accordingly, e.g. "It was a bright and sunny morning and little wisps of clouds were floating in the sky. Then the clouds joined up and got bigger and heavier and large drops of rain fell from them. Then there was a great flash of light and a clap of thunder. When the storm was over the sun came out and the clouds became light and wispy and then they vanished altogether."